Millennium Liturgy

D1455663

Christopher Byworth

Rector of St Helens

GROVE BOOKS LIMITED
RIDLEY HALL RD CAMBRIDGE CB3 9HU

Contents

The Cover Illustration is by Peter Ashton

First Impression July 1999
ISSN 0144-1728
ISBN 1 85174 407 X

1

Introduction

'Help! The millennium is almost upon me and I will have to produce lots of creative liturgy and lots of new services, and not just for my church but for special civic and ecumenical occasions!' If this is your feeling as you pick this up, you may be pleased or perplexed because the booklet tries to do both more and less than this. 'Less' because there are no full-blown texts ready for reproduction; but 'more' because resources, including some actual texts, are listed and the more fundamental practical and theological questions are addressed.

This booklet is intended for ministers and others thinking about millennium worship. Clearly all who read it will be in differing situations with differing worship plans. What the booklet seeks to do is first to look at some of the major theological issues that arise and then to look at the three emphases that have been accepted by Churches Together in England (CTE) under the logo 'NewStart.'[1] These three headings are:

1. *NewStart for the World's Poor*: this focuses especially on the Jubilee 2000 campaign which aims at removing or greatly reducing the vast, unrepayable debt of some third world countries to the West. Clearly a lot more than liturgy is envisaged here, but services could play a part and issues such as repentance and restitution would arise.
2. *NewStart at Home* has two thrusts: family life and the local community. Both of these emphases could find liturgical expression and probably should. Both involve ethical questions. Those who are not avowed Christians might well want to be present and probably should be invited to be at a service which majored on these themes. The famous Millennium Resolution might or might not feature in such services.[2]
3. *NewStart with God* lends itself to liturgical occasions, though if evangelism is intended as a high priority, too much insistence on 'you come and join us in church or even in the open air' would not be the most effective way to reach most dechurched or unchurched people.

The overall task of the churches in the millennium is stated by CTE to be: 'to forge a link in people's minds between the year 2000, the name of Jesus Christ

---

1 There are three A4 fold out leaflets on the the three NewStart themes: *NewStart for the World's Poor* 10 for £2.50; *NewStart at Home* 10 for £2.50; *NewStart with God* 10 for £2.50.
2 Millenium Resolution leaflet, 10 for £2.00 (50 for £5.00). The text of the Resolution is: 'Let there be respect for the earth, peace for its people, love in our lives, delight in the good, forgiveness for past wrongs and from now on a new start.'

and the possibility of personal meaning and public hope.' The link certainly needs forging. One newspaper's survey showed that up to 85% of the population failed to answer the question '2000 years after what?' correctly in so far as Jesus' name did not occur in their answer. Christian liturgy has always placed a central focus on Jesus Christ and it must do so with especial emphasis during this of all years.

Finally, resources will play a large part in the usefulness or otherwise of this booklet. Many will be mentioned. They are listed in the footnotes at the bottom of each page. However, CTE were somewhat late in publishing the generally excellent Book One of *Worship Resources for the Millennium*.[3] The crucial Book Two will cover Advent 1999 to Epiphany 2001. The publication date will now be September 1. Its contents have not been seen by the author. Hopefully it will be at least as useful as Book One. Watch out for the review in *News of Liturgy* and if it is positive, buy it quickly!

---

3 *NewStart Worship: Worship Resources for the Millennium*, Book One, £8.00; Book Two will be out, hopefully, by the autumn and cost £12.00. Both books are A4 in plastic ring-binders and can be reproduced.

2

Some Theological Questions

Underlying almost all the proposed services for the millennium are major theological questions which, though not new, are raised sharply by the millennium services that are being suggested. Five of these issues will be tackled in this chapter. There is also some further discussion on questions raised by particular services as they are mentioned in the three following chapters.

How Important to the Christian Faith are Questions of Time and Celebrations of Actual Events?

Paul's words ring out: 'Do not let anyone judge you…with regard to a religious festival, a new moon celebration or a sabbath day. These are a shadow of the things that were to come; the reality, however, is Christ' (Colossians 2.16). There is some dispute on the nature of the false teaching at Colossae which Paul is refuting. But this verse surely refers to Jewish Christians who were wrongly insisting that gentile Christians too must observe Jewish festivals. What Paul might have said about regular festivals for all Christians which celebrate the great Christ events, especially those of Good Friday and Easter, can only be guessed at. My own guess is that he would not have approved of an absolute insistence on them but would have welcomed the emphasis on Christ. On the one hand the primitive church, after the Jerusalem Council, saw the gospel as international (Colossians 3.11; Galatians 3.26–29) and so not tied to Jewish customs, though much deference was to be given to the 'weaker brother.' On the other hand the first day of the week grew quickly into the main day for worship (1 Corinthians 16.2; Acts 20.7; Revelation 1.10) and its link to Jesus' resurrection and his early appearances to his disciples, especially in the context of meals, can hardly have been coincidental. Certainly a yearly celebration of Easter and Good Friday entered early church practice quite quickly.

But 25th–31st December is almost certainly the wrong time of year, and as there was no year 0, 2001 (not 2000) will be year of Christ's 2000th birthday. In addition he was certainly born before the death of Herod the Great in 4 BC, so that the 2000th anniversary is long past. All of this has to be conceded, but the pragmatic point is decisive. This is when our world is going to celebrate the 2000th anniversary. As churches we either do it now or miss the boat altogether evangelistically. And it might not be very easy for all the churches to agree when else to celebrate, having missed almost certainly the actual double millennium and with eastern and western Christendom still divided over when to celebrate Easter and, to a lesser extent, Christmas.

At a deeper level, the celebration of God's decisive saving acts in history has always been part of the Jewish faith and, arguably, the Christian faith too. Passover celebrates the greatest of God's deliverances for Jews, the Exodus from Egypt and the start of both the promised nation and the promised land. Purim remembers Esther's rescue of her exiled people from virtual genocide. Hanukkah looks back to 164 BC and Judas Maccabeus' rededication of the temple and its altar after their desecration by Antiochus Epiphanes. Christians focus especially on Christ's birth, death and resurrection. The incarnation happens at a particular time and place, and just the right one for the rapid growth and expansion of a new world faith. It was a *'kairos'* indeed (Galatians 4.4). *'Kairos'* means not just a moment in time but a unique moment of opportunity. Christians have always and rightly emphasized this particularity of place and time, a point to be discussed more fully in the next section. Jesus 'was crucified under Pontius Pilate' as the early creeds made clear. There is a balance over the importance of both time and, to a lesser extent, place for the Christian. On the one hand we want to say 'all time is holy' and 'in Christ the emphasis must be on holy people rather than holy land or holy temple.' On the other hand, the sending of Christ, God's greatest salvation act, came at a particular point in time and place just as God comes still to us by his Spirit at a particular place and time. We want to echo both the things the angel said at the tomb: 'He is not here...he is risen' and 'Come, see the place.'

How Big a Part Does History Play in God's Self-revelation and Do We Have a Broadly Accurate Record of the History of Jesus on Which to Base Our Celebrations?

These are huge questions and only the sketchiest of answers can be given. The classic Christian faith sees time as linear with a beginning and an end. It is not an endless circle. Indeed, history is His Story. God starts everything off. Creation is *'ex nihilo,'* 'from nothing,' a Big Bang. God will also end this world as we know it as he superimposes his other order completely upon this order. Into that time line God has intervened decisively in normative acts of self-revelation. He did this first in the history of his ancient people the Jews and then supremely and finally in the climax of their history with the coming of God's kingdom in Jesus' life, death and resurrection. Christians now live in the overlap of the 'ages' in the 'now but not yet' of God's final reign or kingdom. This story is their theology and it is in essence historical. Because of this it is not only natural but totally appropriate to celebrate those key revelatory events regularly and especially at times like a 2000th anniversary. Were we not commanded: 'Do this in remembrance of me'? In the context of the Last Supper that command referred primarily to remembering Jesus' death and resurrection.

The question of the historicity of the gospel accounts of Jesus' life has created a vast and ongoing literature. The recent trend among most scholars has been to find more rather than less history as we learn ever more about the many faces of first century Judaism.[4] Archaeology has also played its part, and a uniformly positive one. Obviously particular sayings or events in Jesus' life cannot be proved or disproved by archaeology, but the tendency of the findings has been to support the cultural world pictured by the gospels. Far from giving a later, anachronistic picture, we can now make increasing sense of more and more parts of the gospel texts. New Testament scholars and archaeologists, of all persuasions, are increasingly working together with positive results. In a Grove Biblical booklet due out towards the end of this year (B 13), Howard Marshall will review the state of play in 'historical Jesus' studies. Clearly a miraculous event such as a resurrection cannot be proven nor can the particular interpretation that Jesus put upon his own coming death. But regarding the resurrection, it can (and in my view largely has) been demonstrated that there is compelling evidence for the New Testament's belief in the resurrected Jesus as a renewed and supraphysical person alive again in a new dimension. On the way Jesus saw the significance of his death, we can say that his interpretation makes sense of most of his sayings and actions in that final week. It is also likely to be Jesus' own interpretation rather than the Gospel writers' because it is both a distinct development from contemporary Jewish messianic expectation, and sufficiently unlike the early church's later understanding. Thus it can hardly be merely the view of the evangelists which they have read back into the earlier events from their own later and more developed theology.

So history is central to the Christian understanding of God's self-revelation and it is possible and right to make historical assertions about the greatest teachings and events in the life of Jesus. To celebrate those teachings and events in a special way in the year 2000 is not only natural but in a sense demanded by our theology.

What Does Christian Remembering Involve Especially in an Act of Worship?

Clearly any specifically millennium service will have an element of looking back; but are there constraints on how this should be done and what should be included? Certainly there is much in Christian history, and that of most churches and their local communities, to say sorry for. This could well be a sensitive issue and it is explored further in the chapter on NewStart at home. There should also be a looking forward—an essential commitment in the present to do something, under God, to start to achieve what the local church and even community believe to be God's plan for their future. All of this would fit well into a Renewal of the Covenant type of service such as Methodism uses annually or can be found

---

4   Recent books on Jesus (relevant also for chapter 4): S Neill and N T Wright, *The Interpretation of the New Testament 1861–1986* (OUP); E P Sanders, *The Historical Figure of Jesus* (Allen Lane); J Dominic Crossan, *Jesus: A Revolutionary* (San Francisco: Harper); Ben Witherington, *The Jesus Quest* (IVP); Tom Wright, *The Original Jesus* (short, popular and good) (Lion); Tom Wright, *Jesus and the Victory of God* (massive and learned) (SCM).

in some Scottish Watchnight services.

Christian remembering has always been more than just casting your mind back. The Jewish approach to Passover was carried forward into the Christian eucharist with its central: 'Do this in remembrance of me.' The aim here is to make the past so real that the force of that past event, in this case Jesus' death and resurrection, makes an impact now on the worshipping believer. In one sense the event is relived. Christian baptism is likewise an entering into Christ's death and resurrection: 'We were therefore buried with him through baptism into death, in order that, just as Christ was raised from the dead through the glory of the Father, we too may live a new life.' (Romans 6.4). Considerable imagination and a bold use of symbols will be needed to convey all of that. Peter Atkins in chapter seven of his *Worship 2000!* has some good examples.[5]

How then are we to remember? Scripture has much to say on this subject and the classic passage is surely Deuteronomy 6.1–9.6. Here Moses warns Israel not to forget God's goodness when they enter and take possession of the promised land. They are not to look back in conceit as if it had been their efforts that achieved all this (7.7; 8.17, 18; 9.4–6). Self congratulation needs to be markedly absent from services celebrating a church's history or the history of their town, village or city. Glory is to be clearly given to God for worthy achievements. A careful balance will be needed since, more positively, other passages urge us to find inspiration from the great men and women of God from our past (Hebrews 11.1–12.3). The final focus, as in Hebrews, should always fall on Jesus. Lessons are to be learned for the present (1 Corinthians 10.1–12; Acts 7; Luke 20.9–19). Repentance now for the past is never far away (see chapter three); and if our past has been 'good,' then the challenge comes to remember our first love and do the things we did at first (Revelation 2.1–7) or else God warns of judgment (Deuteronomy 7.4; Revelation 3.16).

What of our attitude to the future? Certainly a cocksure, supposedly Victorian, 'every day in every way I get better and better' is excluded. We, like the Israelites, are warned that progress may be slow (Deuteronomy 7.22). But we are not to grow despondent. Troubles can be a sign of God's testing (Deuteronomy 7.17; 8.3–6). We are not to be afraid but to show a quiet confidence in God's provision (Deuteronomy 7.9; 8.7–10) . The New Testament in part transfers this victory to the next life (Romans 8.28–39) but also assures us that 'the gates of Hades will not overcome' God's church (Matthew 16.18), a promise endorsed by church history.

Christian remembering will therefore lie at the heart of millennium worship; but it will need handling with sensitivity, humility and imagination. There will be both sober reflection and perhaps acts of penitence for the past. There will be a naming of lessons to be learned now and a quiet trust in God and committed

5 Peter Atkins. *Worship 2000!* (Fount: Harper Collins. 1999. 210pp. £12.99).

determination to bring about more of his kingdom for our church and town in the future.

How Far and in What Ways Can Christian Worship Also Embrace Those Who Make No Profession of the Christian Faith?

Civic services and multi-faith acts of worship have long raised this question. The new Resolution if used in Christian worship will raise the issue afresh, precisely because of what it omits. Of course those without an avowed Christian faith have long been attending the occasional service. But that is not the same as the church devising acts of worship that avoid the name or worship of Christ. The Church of England, for example, has steadfastly refused to write a funeral service that does not major on Christ and the Christian hope. Charitable assumption is used for all the departed. Should this be the way forward for those churches that are planning multi-faith acts appropriate to their local communities? Or can multi- or even non-faith 'services' be written and used with sensitivity and integrity? Certainly Peter Atkins has attempted one such in his Spirit service in chapter seven of *Worship 2000!* It succeeds in many ways but the author of this booklet confesses to remaining unconvinced. Why is this?

Worship is surely directed towards God and Christian worship towards the Christian God which means God as he has supremely revealed himself to us in Jesus, the God-man. What made the first Jewish Christian worship so distinctive was precisely its worship of Christ. This can be seen in the preservation in Aramaic of the prayer '*maranatha*' which means, 'Come, Lord,' that is, 'Lord Jesus.' Jesus is already being hailed as 'Lord,' the title for Yahweh in the Old Testament and the commonest title for most gods in the Graeco-Roman world then—Lord Serapis, Lord Osiris and even Lord Caesar. Paul writes accurately: 'For even if there are so-called gods...(as indeed there are many "gods" and many "lords"), yet for us there is but one God, the Father...and there is but one Lord, Jesus Christ...' (1 Corinthians 8.6). The distinctive first 'creed' was 'Jesus is Lord' (1 Corinthians 12.3; Romans 10.9). Christians 'recite a form of words to Christ as a god,' Pliny tells us in north-west Turkey around 110 AD (Pliny, *Epistles* 10:96:7). Hymns to Christ had been sung for some time before that. Philippians 2.6–11 is widely believed by scholars to be at least based on a pre-Pauline hymn to Jesus. That would date it in the 40s AD and make it amongst the earliest fragments in the New Testament. Thomas' falling at the feet of the risen Christ and calling him 'my Lord and my God' (John 20.29) is merely a narrative example of what the first Christians did when they worshipped distinctively together. Presumably they also celebrated a communion meal whose centre was the worship and experience of the living Christ.

If this is the distinctive feature of early Christian worship, it cannot be left out or played down in any service that claims to be Christian and, least of all, in the millennium year! However, that is not to say that people from all faiths and none could not be asked to be present, though of course it should be made clear that it is an act of explicitly Christian worship to which they are being invited. In my view it would also be possible to hold other gatherings which would not be called Christian and which would not be worship in that the deity, though acknowledged, was not directly addressed. At such a gathering the Resolution could be said together with integrity. However the Millennium Resolution Litany on page 18 of Book One of *Worship Resources for the Millennium* would probably be a bridge too far, for it addresses God as 'Lord.' The author is Rector at a parish church in a traditional south Lancashire town where almost all are from a similar culture and where town hall and the church have close relationships and mutual trust and almost all are nominally Christian. In such (easy) circumstances, Millennium civic services, like other ones, can and will be explicitly Christian and are unlikely to cause any tremors. However, this issue is unlikely to be so uncontroversial everywhere!

How Far Should Our Worship Engage with People's Hopes and Longings for the Future and Their Seeing the Millennium as the Dawn of a New Age?

Some see the new millennium as far more than just an excuse for a massive party. They long for a new age, a new start. Hence the relevance of CTE's slogan. The significance of special numbers has something to do with it. 30th, 60th, 70th and especially 100th birthdays are special. A few people even get excited when their car's milometer clocks 10,000 or even 100,000. This is Christ's 2000th birthday. We can surely build on that. New Year's Eve will bring, for some, deep longings for a renewed earth ecologically, a world renewed in peace and love, and a new age of justice and plenty. Christian worship could respond to and build on that. Christ as God's word and wisdom in creation should be emphasized. There is a strong case for the use of Celtic-style creation material. God's entry into our created world at the incarnation is another linked truth. Above all Christ's cross and resurrection redeem and renew creation and the whole cosmos (Romans 8.22–25).

There is a strong look forward for many people at this time and it is associated with the millennium. Christians too believe in a millennium, that hard to interpret one in Revelation 20.1–6. Too often cranky understandings have led us to avoid it. But Michael Gilbertson's excellent booklet shows that four great truths for the future are taught here: the triumph of God; the Lordship of Christ; God's vindication of his people; and God's commitment to transform the earth.[6] The great Christian hope of Christ's return and a new heaven and a new earth could be among our most relevant truths to meet many longings at this time. Advent 1999 should become especially poignant.

---

6 Michael Gilbertson, *The Meaning of the Millennium* (Grove Biblical Series No 5, Cambridge: Grove Books).

3
NewStart for the World's Poor

It is, hopefully, a commonplace by now that Christians should have a special concern for the world's poor—though some may still need persuading. More may need persuading that this concern needs expressing in worship. Worship resources from Christian Aid, TEAR Fund, CAFOD and others have meant that many, perhaps most, churches in Britain are used to at least an annual service on this theme.[7] For the millennium there should be significantly more emphasis than this. There is to be a special stress on breaking the chains of third world debt, much of which is unrepayable and is crippling welfare expenditure in some of the poorest countries. Some end up repaying the west far more in a year than they receive in aid. The campaign that coordinates this effort is called *Jubilee 2000*. I will briefly examine the theology behind it and seek to give some examples of how such things could be expressed in a service, as well as pointing to further resources.

Theological Basis
It is not hard to establish a biblical and theological basis for a special concern for the world's poor nor a reason why the millennium is a particularly appropriate time to express and seek to do something concrete about some aspect of it. Much theological writing has sought to show that the God of the Bible has a 'bias to the poor.'[8] The apostate emperor, Julian, acknowledged ruefully in 362 AD that the 'the impious Galileans support not only their own poor but ours as well (while) all men see that our people (that is, fellow pagans who support the Roman state) lack aid from us' (Julian, *Epistle 49*, 429C–432A). Such was the enviable reputation of the fourth century church among its ardent opponents. Would that ours was similar!

But why a special effort and special liturgy just because this is 2000 AD? That too can be answered by Scripture when the Jewish concept of jubilee is examined. This idea grew from an extension of the sabbath principle of one day's rest in seven. The principle was extended from daily life into agriculture so that there was to be no ploughing of the land in the seventh year. Instead it

---

7   Agencies: *Christian Aid*, PO Box 100, London SE1 7RT Tel: (Debt material) 0171-523-2248, (general) 0171-523-2229; *CAFOD*, Romero Close, Stockwell Road, London SW9 9TY Tel: 0171-733-7900, Fax: 0171-274-9630; *Tear Fund*, 100 Church Road, Teddington TW11 8QE Tel: 0895-355-8355; *Jubilee 2000 Coalition*, PO Box 100, London SE1 7RT Tel: 0171-401-9999, Fax: 0171-401-3999.
8   David Sheppard, *Bias to the Poor* (chapter one for the theology) (Hodders, 1983). Archbishop's Commission, *Faith in the City* (chapter three) (Church House Publishing, 1985). Many more resources are listed in the CTE leaflet *NewStart for the World's Poor*.

'rested.' Part of the reason for this was 'then the poor among your people may get food from it' (Exodus 23.10–12). Leviticus 25.8–17 develops the sabbath rest principle into a sabbath of sabbaths so that every fiftieth year (about once a lifetime in their life-expectancy terms) should be consecrated and 'liberty should be proclaimed throughout the land to all its inhabitants. It shall be a jubilee for you; each one of you is to return to his family property and each to his own clan…in this Year of Jubilee everyone is to return to his own property..' (Leviticus 25.10, 13). In other words, debt-slavery was to be abolished at least once in everyone's lifetime. The term 'Jubilee' comes from the Hebrew word *'yobel'* meaning a 'ram's horn.' Of such was the trumpet used to herald this year of thanksgiving for property reverting to its original owner, of debts remitted and Hebrew slaves freed. The modern campaign to cancel the worst and most unrepayable debts of the poorest countries to the richest fits snugly indeed into this biblical command. Here is warrant, surely, for debt cancellation and celebration worship to praise the just and loving God whose idea this was and is.

Celebration or Protest?

Clearly Jubilee 'services' would be celebrating what had already happened or was about to happen, though one may wonder whether this Old Testament ideal was always lived up to in practice. Nehemiah 10.31 and 1 Maccabees 4 show that this was practised, at least sometimes, after the return from exile. Such are the difficulties and prevarications today that it will be miraculous indeed if any really significant change of heart and practice comes over the G7 countries and the International Monetary Fund before the end of 2000 AD. In this situation of nothing or very little to celebrate, what liturgy would be appropriate? Might not an even shriller, prophetic protest be more appropriate? That will almost certainly continue to be needed. But so will the continued education of our Western, church-going public and for this purpose special services have a part to play alongside petitions, badges, picketing G7 conferences and the rest. Could it not be argued, though, that worship is directed mainly at God and that he needs no reminding of this appalling evil? 'Protest and action "yes" but worship "no!"' This need not be a dichotomy. All worship includes an element of God speaking to us and our listening. The message in the service could be a clear, prophetic one. Maybe the temple sacrifices and great festivals were the setting where some of the Old Testament prophets made their voices heard. Jesus seems to have done just that when his parabolic action of cleansing (or rather of briefly preventing) the temple's sacrificial system, spoke of God's coming judgment on all that Judaism then stood for. He did this in the context of Israel's greatest act of worship, the Passover.

One more difficult issue looms when considering a new start for the world's poor. How far are we responsible for making them poor and encouraging them rashly to take out loans they would not be able to repay? Are not many of the poor's problems a reflection of the way the G7 countries largely run the world's economy? Could it not be argued that we are all, north and south alike, responsible for continuing to pollute and degrade God's natural world? And are there not also a range of other 'systemic' evils for which we must at least take part of the blame? Is not ethnic cleansing one of them? Worse still, could it not be argued that some of the great evils of the past—the crusades, apartheid, slavery, colonial domination, the exploitation of workers by bosses, the suppression of women and racism for example—have left a legacy among us especially felt by those who were not so long ago, and may even still, be the oppressed? Even church history is littered with acts of oppression by one group or denomination over another. There may be sensitivities in your own area on this point. Anglicans having been traditionally the most powerful church in Britain have perhaps the most soul-searching to do. A new start for the world's poor and 'at home' will involve all of us in repentance. So the question arises how best to express this in liturgy.

Resources for Reconciliation

Perhaps the best feature of the Churches Together in England's publication *Worship Resources for the Millennium* Book One is its section on this issue. Pages 8 to 11 deal with reconciliation and repentance in a tender way as practical preparation is made for an act of worship on this theme. However, there are difficulties, especially with confessing the sins of the more distant past. Can we authentically say sorry when we were not personally involved and to whom on earth should this be said anyway? Can most Germans or Japanese for example be expected to go on saying sorry to the World War Two allies or should we in Britain go on apologizing to the Germans for the bombing of Dresden and other atrocities? Sometimes amends can be made. Right now a huge, golden sceptre and orb has been made by many English firms from donations. It will stand on the rebuilt Frauenkirche in Dresden. That surely is appropriate! Another problem with apologizing for the distant past is the need to recognize that cultures differ and moral standards alter with the centuries. British overseas missions might well now be seen as having had mixed motives and being at least partly tarnished by colonialism, but would it have appeared in that light then? Should we apologize for things that our predecessors would not, for the most part, even have seen as wrong? Another example could be industrial pollution at the height of the industrial revolution. Where a sin goes unrecognized over one or many generations, as slavery did for so long, and where it is clear biblically that it has been a sin all along, then penitence is surely right. But there needs to be near consensus and biblical warrant that we are wiser than our forefathers. Often it may be that they knew more of right and wrong than we do. One final problem needs looking at: how to make restitution if the sin is still affecting our contemporaries badly today. Only sensitive consultation can ascertain if that is so. Symbolic acts in the context of worship could bring real healing, but a lot of thought and preparation will be needed before any texts are composed.

Finally, what should be the content of such a service? The right ingredients would seem to be these. First, a strong assertion of God's compassion and justice from Scripture and in song. Secondly, a highlighting of the injustice or need. A lot of imagination could be used here with video, telephone and so many powerful and immediate means of communication. An interview with someone directly affected can make a big impact. There will need to be an expression of penitence and, if possible and appropriate, some act or symbol of restitution. An opportunity to respond to need and/or to protest against injustice needs to be part of the service, and hopefully this would be more than just a collection. Why could not your Member of Parliament be present and questioned briefly? Clearly intercessory prayers must play a large part. There are now, from the aid agencies, many resources for worship and the final section of this booklet will list some of them. The CTE Worship Book One has material addresssing the question of the uprooted and homeless. Peter Atkins' *Worship 2000!* has a useful selection of themes, readings and prayers. The Jubilee 2000 office can supply material for worship on the particular theme of third world debt.

What time of year should such a service or services be held? There are some obvious points in the year. New Year itself would be appropriate. It would strike the note of the world's poor early on and New Year's resolutions that are easily made and easily broken would make a powerful message. The Resolution itself should be fresh in all minds then and its line 'peace for its people and forgiveness for past wrongs' would lend itself to such a service. Christian Aid Week is the next obvious point—though if repentance was to be the major feature any Sunday in Lent could be good. A Sunday around the time when the G7 countries meet and Harvest are two other obvious times. There could be so much going on in your church or area that your choice is limited. The major thing to ensure is that this does not just slip past as yet another Christian Aid or Harvest service. This vital theme needs emphasis and special treatment—perhaps two Sundays or a whole series of sermons and services!

4

NewStart at Home

Some of the most useful publications for the millennium are the three fold-out A4 leaflets produced by the Churches Together in England. There is one for each of the three NewStart areas. It is probably significant that whereas the other two have plenty of material to cover six sides, NewStart at Home only fills four sides. One of these four pages is rightly dedicated to resources but even here there is little, if anything, to help the budding liturgist. Peter Atkins' book has nothing to offer and CTE's own Book One of *Worship Resources* has only a bare three pages that are directly relevant, though other material could be pressed into service.

There is also the danger of confusion. 'At Home' is clearly understood to have two different meanings, both of which are being promoted for the millennium year and both of which could and should find liturgical expression. First, under the question: 'What kind of Britain—our national home—do we want for the new century?' the area of home and family life is opened up. 'Where do we need to make a new start in our homes—our families, our personal values, our areas of "brokenness"?' This question remains unanswered and unlooked at in the rest of the leaflet. However, in CTE's *Worship Resources* for 'at home' the whole three pages focus on home and family and the second meaning is ignored. The second meaning for, 'at Home' refers to life in Britain at large and the examples given suggest, wisely, a special focus on the issues particularly relevant to your own local city, town or village. In this chapter, both meanings will be looked at and questions raised and ideas for worship will be provided, though not texts as such.

Homes and Family Life

Obvious questions need to be faced in this area. An ever smaller number of people and percentage of church-goers live in a family with two parents and young children. An ever larger proportion live as single people in one-person flats or houses. This is due to two main factors. We live longer and that means more widowers and even more widows. Marriages break up and our living-together liaisons break up even more quickly, as do second marriages. All of this has meant an increasing need for more housing units even though the population is not increasing overall. There is certainly disagreement too as to whether a single parent home is as good for the child or children as having two parents living with them. Grandparents and nurseries increasingly do the caring as one or both parents return to work.

In this situation, how far is seeing the local church as a family a helpful emphasis and how far is the term 'father' a helpful one to use of God for many non-churchgoers and even churchgoers? The Bishop of Liverpool talks of God, usually, not as just 'father' but almost always as 'the good father.' In Anglican church circles what used to be called 'Family Services' or 'Family Communions' are increasingly being called 'All-Age Services' or 'All-Age Eucharists' or simply 'Services of the Word.' However, the author doubts whether we should abandon the family concept so quickly. Is it not better to try and redeem so biblical an image? Is it one that can still communicate well today? Surely the classic Anglican position on this, as on so much else, should be that 'abuse must not stop right use.' The family metaphor is deeply biblical. It expresses the relationship between the first two persons of the Holy Trinity. The Father-Son language is used throughout to express God's relationship to his people; and 'daughter' can be used as well. Interestingly in the Johannine literature, the term 'Son' is reserved for Jesus, presumably to highlight his uniqueness and the category difference between his relationship to the Father and ours. In John's writings Christians are always 'children' not 'sons' or 'daughters.'

Whatever we call services involving those of all ages, the issue of family life should be very high on our agendas for the millennium year and for long after that. The extended family was clearly the social pattern in both Old and New Testament times. Even a watered down atomic family, the modern western version, often has more to commend it than today's alternatives. This is certainly true as an environment in which children can grow up securely. Parenting courses are increasingly popular and an excellent evangelistic contact point for churches with the de-churched. Marriage preparation is perhaps less significant. Fewer are marrying in churches and it is increasingly hard to get couples to attend in advance. Marriage reinforcement later and discussion courses for the divorced and separated are often welcomed.

How can all of this be given both liturgical expression and special emphasis in this year? CTE's Book One does have ideas for Annunciation services, though the millennium flavour is not especially prominent. Any of the feasts for the Blessed Virgin Mary would make a convenient excuse. Holy Family Sunday would be another good day. Mothering Sunday has long been a popular folk festival. Could Father's Day in June also be pressed into service? Valentine's Day is the most obvious time of all both for engaged couples and married folk perhaps wanting to renew their vows. The renewing of vows and blessing of rings (or even the couple wearing the rings!) could be highlighted in a service at the end of a short course on marriage enhancement. It may be possible to lay on such services in cooperation with RELATE,[9] CRUSE or other secular agencies both for marrieds and for single-parent families. Church schools or those where the local church has an *entrée* are other obvious link points. Most dioceses have

9   *RELATE*. Herbert Gray College. Little Church Street. Rugby CV21 3AP Tel: 01788-573241.

an officer for marriage and family life. (S)he will probably know of further resources including liturgical ones.

Life in the Community

The other meaning of 'at home' is 'in the community' which primarily means in the local community. Liaising with the local authority especially over one or more special services is the obvious thing to do. CTE is encouraging every town, city and village up and down the country to hold a civic service on Sunday 2nd January at around 2.30pm. This raises several questions.

- First, how explicitly Christian should such a service be? See the last chapter for some consideration of this. In most situations, the Resolution could probably be used and spoken about. In many places the Christian content would be sufficiently acceptable also to allow the use of CTE's litany on the Resolution (see Book One, page 20f).
- Second, how wide a civic area should be covered and in which church building should the service be held? Maybe better, should it be held in a public, secular building such as the Town Hall? The problem here is that parish boundaries and local authority ones do not always coincide. A local authority may not know which church to relate to even if it wants to cooperate. Much will depend on relationships between clergy and key town hall officials. It may be possible to function at a smaller level—village parish council or local ward. The quality of the church–civic links already made will probably prove decisive.
- Third, how ecumenically wide can this service be? Clearly, if ever there was a case for total, ecumenical cooperation, it is now. Indeed, much more for the whole millennium could be achieved, if there is a high level of cooperation. This is especially true of NewStart with God, dealt with in the next chapter.
- Fourth, who should be invited? The aim must be to get as wide a cross-section of the 'movers and shakers' in your area as possible, as well as a lot of the general public and ordinary churchgoers. MPs, the MEP, Ward Councillors and key executive officers from the town hall or parish council are the first target. The commerce and business world are, notoriously, often the least responsive. Key shop managers and small industries can be contacted through the local Chamber of Commerce. The caring agencies often do respond. Health, the Police, schools, youth and adult training and colleges and the whole range of voluntary organizations most easily accessed normally through your local Community Voluntary Services office. Clearly representatives of all the main Christian denominations should be invited and perhaps other faith communities also. The Christian content can be made plain and people not wanting to come can always turn down the invitation.

The theme could have a 'look back' element. In part this would say sorry and celebrate (see chapter two); but the main element would be a concern for community issues now. Here are some ideas for themes:[10]

- the growing gap between the 'haves' and the 'have nots';
- the increasing breakdown in family life (see above);
- a high level of abortion and alcohol and drug abuse and unemployment;
- a degree of racism beneath the surface of society;
- an ever-rising prison population;
- an ageing population and the availability of good health care;
- self-confidence and dignity for the more under-privileged.

There should be a clearly local flavour. This demands a focus on the one or two issues felt to be most relevant.

A larger concern is whether there should be any act of commitment and, if so, what its nature should be. If the content is basically Christ-centred, then this could take the less direct form of a litany (see CTE's Book One pages 18, 19). If a clearer spoken commitment is desirable, then a question and answer form could be used.

The shape of the service could be past, then future and finally present as at many Watchnight services and as in CTE Book One pages 24–29. Such a shape would be especially appropriate at the start of the millennium year, for instance at a 2nd January service. The 'future' section could tie in with plans the borough may be making for the next decade. Better still, there could be a section expressing the community's dreams about how they would like to see their town/village/city in 20 years time. That could be shared and then prayed over. The obvious place for an act of civic commitment would be at the end of the service. Perhaps an annual meeting or even service plus meeting to review progress could be agreed for future years!

Each local authority will almost certainly already have plans for the year 2000. It may even be the case that there has been church representation in the planning. If so, some of this could more easily be included in the service. Certainly NewStart at Home should involve the churches in far more than just one civic service. The presence of key clergy and lay people at many of the village or town's civic millennium events will probably be welcome. How extensive these are will depend on the size of the budget and the degree of organizing that is already in place or not.

One new idea which may be tried here by the Town Hall came from an ecumenical church initiative and received funding and administrative back-up

---

10 *The Common Good* (Catholic Church's Social Teaching, 1996) £3.00 from Gabriel Communications Ltd, First floor, St James' Buildings, Oxford Street, Manchester M1 6FP Tel: 0161-236-8856. Many more resources are listed in the CTE leaflet *NewStart at Home*.

from the Town Hall. It is called: 'I have a dream.' This encourages any individuals, but preferably groups from any and every part of the town's life, to submit something audio and/or visual of what their vision for the town is for the year 2020. It may be called '2020 Vision'! These 'dreams' are to be selected and mounted in a prominent position in the town centre in a marquee for a week. Prizes are awarded by a local panel, a video is made of the best of them and one or more meetings are held towards the end of the year so that the public can ask sharp questions about implementation to those in positions from where they could help make at least some of the dreams come true. The churches will be asked to supply their vision for what the town might look like if it became more Christ-centred. Whether or not this idea appeals or is possible, the concept of a forward look in any civic service for the millennium year is crucial.

5
NewStart with God

The declared aim of the NewStart project is stated in all the CTE literature in these words: 'The task of the churches in the Millennium is to forge a link in people's minds between the year 2000, the name of Jesus Christ and the possibility of personal meaning and public hope.' Of the three NewStart headings, a NewStart with God has perhaps the priority. But is it just evangelism and how is evangelism to be defined anyway these days? The current emphasis on evangelism as a process rather than a moment opens up the question as to when, if ever in this life, a person has been fully evangelized. Certainly the 'renewal' (and that word too has a wide range of meanings) of both individuals and churches is often closely associated with evangelism so that a new start with God could be interpreted as church renewal also. Indeed the excellent fold-out leaflet with this title from CTE offers a very broad range of ideas across this whole spectrum. Another excellent booklet, full of useful ideas, is Michael Rees, *Celebrating the Millennium in the Local Church*.[11]

The difficulty of worship events in this context, unless the prime focus is the renewal of Christians, is that they will be 'in-drag' events rather than outreach ones. By their nature they will be based on the presupposition of 'you come to us' rather than 'we go out to you.' Almost all the evidence available suggests that however imaginatively an event is laid on, however low its cringe factor for the non-church person, only about 20% of those who go will be wholly estranged from church life. Of that 20% few will come unless a Christian friend has prayed much for them and invited them. So the main thrust in outreach will not be worship events of any kind, not even those held on non-church premises. Read other booklets on evangelism if outreach is your main aim! Probably the main kind of event to lay on for 'outsiders' is a fun gathering with low gospel content where visitors will hopefully gain the impression that 'God is good and Christians are OK.'[12] So what place is there for a chapter on worship under this heading?

However true the above emphasis is, unchurched or dechurched people do still come to church occasionally. Clergy, and particularly Anglicans, probably contact more people through funerals, infant baptisms and (perhaps now to a lesser extent) weddings than through all the special events they ever lay on. Also, in some areas, people do still come into church on the odd Sunday morn-

---

11 Michael Rees, *Celebrating the Millennium in the Local Church* (Grove Evangelism Series No 39, Cambridge: Grove Books).
12 Laurence Singlehurst, *Sowing, Reaping, Keeping* (chapter 3) (Crossway).

ing for no very obvious reason and others will come from time to time with churchgoing friends. These opportunities to befriend and to present something of Christ must not be missed. Perhaps the most important ingredient here is not a user-friendly liturgy but a sensitive welcome. *Fanfare for a New Generation* is an inter-church organization that seeks to promote this.[13] It has ten goals to help churches become more welcoming, relevant and challenging:

1. We will make you welcome.
2. We will be family friendly.
3. We will make sure you can hear clearly.
4. We will be practical and relevant.
5. We will help you explore answers to your deepest questions.
6. We will offer you time to stop and think in a busy life.
7. We will help you make sense of the Bible and who Jesus is.
8. We will make sure your visit will be helpful and challenging.
9. We will help you discover for yourself God's love, acceptance and forgiveness.
10. We will offer you the chance to make a new start.

Fanfare also offers resources to turn this dream into greater reality.

There are many ways in which our buildings can also be more welcoming. Noticeboards could be given a face-lift and a special one erected. Many churches of all denominations in some districts are erecting the same cheap but attractive board with the slogan: 'The Millennium is CHRIST'S 2000th BIRTHDAY. Worship Him here—now.'[14] All churches with bells are encouraged to ring them on Saturday 1st January at noon. Floodlighting the church building and/or erecting a lit cross on a tower are all ideas that are being tried. Opening the building, and not just at noon on 1st January, may be a possibility for some despite security risks and manpower shortages. Using the building for concerts, exhibitions, flower festivals, lunchtime lectures and much else will be appropriate in some places though impossible in others.

Services by Churches Together

Before looking at what special services might be offered by individual churches, it is worth considering what and how much can be done ecumenically together. In his final prayer in John 17, Jesus not only prayed for unity between believers but wanted it 'so that the world may believe that you [the Father] have sent me...' (John 17.21). It is a good witness when Christians clearly cooperate. Unity Week would be an early opportunity and some may even hold

---

13 *Fanfare for a New Generation*, 115 Southwark Bridge Road, London SE1 0AX Tel: 0171-450-9070/1, Fax: 0171-450-9060.

14 Manufacturer: Signs of Cheshire, 432 London Road, Davenham, Northwich, Cheshire CW9 8EF Fax: 01606-49916. Price £64.00 (incl VAT) + £9.25 p&p. Delivery 4-6 weeks.

a New Year's Eve united service too. Pentecost has to be the golden opportunity. Peter Atkins' book *Worship 2000!* offers some very imaginative liturgies for Epiphany and Ascension (see chapter 7). The civic service is another obvious candidate and so are services for the world's poor and world debt. The limits are those of energy, goodwill and cooperation rather than of opportunity. It would be even better, of course, to plan together for explicitly evangelistic happenings with presentations, perhaps, rather than services. There may well be district or city-wide events. In England there are two Marches for Jesus on Saturday 10th June in London and Liverpool. There are three more in Glasgow, Belfast and Cardiff. Some areas are planning a special Sunday morning service altogether for Pentecost and abandoning their own main services in order to take part.

Services in Individual Churches

What kind of services might be laid on in our own churches to help us make a new start with God? Once again the aim needs to be clear. Is this mainly a service of rededication for Christians or an outreach to invited 'fringe-type' friends? It will probably be the former. If so, a service early in the year, and possibly on 2nd January itself in the morning, would be appropriate. Material from the Methodist Renewal of the Covenant service is now widely used and could be adapted. Some New Year-style liturgical material is offered in CTE's Book One pages 23–29. Epiphany or the Sunday after would make a good, alternative, early date. If particular faith targets for growth are set by the church council or its equivalent then these could be part of a corporate public commitment made together at the service alongside private and personal resolutions. They could be written out and offered. A service in which these were reviewed later in the year or at the same time next year could also be effective. Other material for recommitment could include a perhaps adapted renewal of baptism vows (the new ones are more explicit) or material adapted from an ordination or induction of clergy or from the licensing of Readers or church leaders.

What should be done on New Year's Eve? Opinions vary widely. CTE's own recommendation is that church people simply join in their family or street parties and bear their witness here. There will, we are told, be a 'millennium moment' of nationwide quiet shortly before midnight. Supposedly all will then light their candles and say the Resolution to themselves. One wonders about the realism of this picture for many reasons. Will all have a candle or have it with them in the pub or at the party? Will all know or want to say silently the Resolution? Will all TV channels carry this moment of silence and will TV be watched by all then? More profoundly, many Christians have expressed a desire to do something more explicitly Christian then. Supposedly there will be no services at that point. In reality many churches and at least one cathedral, Liverpool's Anglican one, will be holding a short and special service then. Town centre churches may well find strangers and regular churchgoers who want to gather inside or outside for the moments around midnight. Quite a number of churches are delivering, to as many homes as they can, not the candle with its holder and Resolution, but a more explicitly Christ-centred gift such as a gospel or a cross. It seems clear that there will be a wide variety of practice and each church will do what it thinks right. Certainly those that do hold midnight services will need to think clearly and imaginatively about them. Probably, they should, above all, be short—no longer than 30 minutes—with a great symbolic act of rejoicing afterwards. This is not the best time to hold the large, one-off service of new start for Christians.

But the problem with symbolic one-off services, however powerful, is precisely that they are one-off. A new start with God might well be better achieved by a whole year of teaching , worship and evangelism focussed on Jesus. Obviously different ideas would meet different needs.

For long-standing Christians, something dealing with modern research and archaeology and Jesus would be stretching. There are recent TV series of varying stances,[15] some quite radical. No doubt there will be more. There are fairly simple books which could be potted and used as a basis for study and discussion. No doubt there will be a good New Testament popularizer somewhere in the area whom you could call on for a series of talks on 'the real Jesus.' How the risen Lord has been seen down the ages both in theology, films, popular culture and art would make a good series. How far do we all tend to make Jesus in our own varying images and how far is that justified or inevitable?

For less learned folk a group Bible study course on Jesus would be good.[16] Notes and questions from a simple gospel commentary could be used by a group if predigested by the clergy. The Bible Society's *Faith comes by Hearing* set of audio tapes of the whole New Testament could be listened to at home by individuals; others might take up the challenge to read a whole gospel at a sitting.[17] Preaching series could work through a gospel, with breaks, using the *Revised Common Lectionary*, Year B.[18] Another series could explore the differing but complementary portrayals of Jesus in the Gospels and the rest of the New Testament. The possibilities are nearly endless.

Concentration on Jesus could also work evangelistically. *The Jesus Video Project* is very interesting.[19] It offers friends and neighbours the 70 minute *Jesus* video free for them to view at home on condition only that they fill in a questionnaire afterwards with a church member. Distributing free gospels, meals with a speaker,

15 ITV's 'The Jesus' Files' with Tony Robinson; Channel Five's 'From Jesus to Christ' with Terry Waite.
16 Leighton Ford, *Meeting Jesus* (Lifebuilder Bible Study Outlines, Scripture Union).
17 Bible Society Tapes series, *Faith Comes by Hearing* (Address above).
18 Revised Common Lectionary in *The Christian Year: Calendar etc* (Church House Publishing).
19 *Jesus Video Project*, Agape, Fairgate House, Kings Road, Tyseley, Birmingham B11 2AA Tel: 0121-765-4404, Fax: 0121-765-4065. Many more resources are listed in CTE's *NewStart with God*.

old-fashioned 'guest services' or lunch-time lectures could all focus on different aspects of Jesus.

The church year makes this focus for churchgoers, but it ends, as far as Jesus is concerned, around Ascension. It could be extended even till Advent in this unique Jesus year. No liturgical texts have been mentioned in this chapter. This is because CTE's Book One already has some seasonal material intended for 1999 but usable for 2000 if it were given a greater millennium flavour. Book Two, published September 1, will have material to cover Advent 1999 till Epiphany 2001. Presumably this will have a strong Jesus and millennium flavour.

A final word of caution may be apposite. Select only a few of these ideas. There will be so much going on in the year 2000 that exhaustion and indigestion could result and lead to fatigue and boredom rather than new understanding, excitement, obedience and commitment. May Christ himself be uplifted in his second millennium year!

6
Some Resources

All of the general resources are available from:

Main CTE Suppliers: Churches Millennium Publications Office
Churches Millennium Enterprises
Church House Bookshop
31 Great Smith Street
London SW1P 3BN

Tel: 0171-340-0276/77 and by credit card
Fax: 0171-799-2717

or   NewStart
c/o Bible Society
Stonehill Green
Westlea
Swindon SN5 7DG

Tel: 01793-418100